TREASURES FROM THE PAST

TREASURES FROM GREECE

David & Patricia Armentrout

The Rourke Book Company, Inc.
Vero Beach, Florida 32964

ACKNOWLEDGEMENT:
The authors would like to thank Marianne Kunnen-Jones and Dr. Brian Rose for their kind assistance in the
preparation of this book.

PHOTO CREDITS:
©Al Michaud: cover, pages 23, 24, 27; ©Galyn C. Hammond: pages 6, 15, 19, 26, 30, 32, 41, 42;
©Susan Alworth: page 20; ©University of Cincinnati/University of Tübingen: pages 11, 16, 18, 29, 33, 37;
©Artville, LLC.: page 4

PRODUCED & DESIGNED by East Coast Studios
eastcoaststudios.com

EDITORIAL SERVICES:
Pamela Schroeder

Library of Congress Cataloging-in-Publication Data

Armentrout, David, 1962-
    Greece: treasures from the past / David and Patricia Armentrout.
        p. cm. — (Treasures from the past)
    Includes index.
    ISBN 1-55916-291-0
    1. Greece—Civilization—Juvenile literature. [1. Greece—Antiquities. 2. Archaeology.] I. Armentrout, Patricia, 1960-
II. Title. III. Treasures from the past (Vero Beach, Fla.)

DF78 .A67 2000
938—dc21
                                                                00–029078

TABLE OF CONTENTS

Greek Treasure 5

Clues and Tools of the Trade 9

The Early Bronze Age 13

Greek Myths and Legends 21

The Legend of Troy.....................................35

Other Ancient Greek Treasures..................39

Glossary...45

Further Reading 47

Index 48

Thessaloniki

GREECE

AEGEAN SEA

IONIAN SEA

Athens

Sparta

CRETE

MEDITERRANEAN SEA

4

GREEK TREASURE

Greece is located in southeastern Europe. Its mainland is the southern most tip of the Balkan *(BALL kin)* peninsula. A peninsula is land that is surrounded by water on three sides. Greece also has islands to the west in the Ionian *(eye OH nee uhn)* Sea and to the east in the Aegean *(eh JEE uhn)* Sea. The largest Greek island is Crete *(KREET),* which is southeast of the mainland. Crete's southern coastline is on the Mediterranean Sea.

The mainland and the islands are very mountainous. Much of Greece is rocky and the soil is poor. Only the small areas of coastal plains are good for farming.

People from around the world love to come to Greece. Millions of tourists visit the mainland and the islands each year. People flock to the beautiful beaches and stroll the many city streets. Tourists spend lots of time eating and drinking at the outdoor taverns and restaurants.

Archaeologists study ancient buildings like this palace on the island of Crete.

TIMELINE

3000 – 2000 BC	Minoan civilizations develop on Crete.
3000 BC	Troy is settled.
3000 BC	Athens is settled.
2000 – 1400 BC	Minoan civilizations on Crete are the center of the Greek world.
1900 BC	Linear A writing develops on Crete.
1700 BC	Minos Palace at Knossos is destroyed by fire.
1600 BC	Mycenae develops on mainland Greece.
1400 – 1000 BC	Linear B writing replaces Linear A. Mycenae is the center of the Greek world.
1200 BC	Agamemnon is King of Mycenae.
1184 BC	Troy is destroyed after 10 years of battling with the Greeks.
750 BC	The Iliad and Odyssey are written by Homer about this time.
776 BC	First Olympic Games are held at Olympia.
550 BC	First plays are performed in Greece. Athens is an important Greek city.
447 BC	The Parthenon is built in Athens.
147 BC	Greece is under Roman Empire rule.

Greece has a rich cultural history that dates back thousands of years. History is another reason why so many people visit Greece. Visitors want to see the **ruins** from the ancient Greek world. The ruins are treasures from past Greek civilizations.

Scientists find the ancient Greek world as interesting as tourists do. An **archaeologist** is a scientist that studies the past. An archaeologist studies past life by studying old remains such as buildings, bridges, or walls. **Artifacts** like jars, statues, and jewelry are also remains. Artifacts and other remains help scientists learn what life was like long ago.

Archaeologists and other scientists also study writings from the past. The ancient Greeks were great writers and thinkers. They used writing as far back as 1400 BC. By about 800 BC, Greek writers kept records and wrote stories and plays. Their stories and poems help explain ancient Greek religion and their way of life. Homer was a Greek poet who lived around 700 BC. He is known for writing two great works called the *Iliad* and the *Odyssey*. His stories have been printed many times over and read worldwide.

Ancient Greek boys went to school and learned arithmetic, reading, and writing. Greek girls stayed home with their mothers and learned to spin and weave wool for clothing.

CLUES AND TOOLS
OF THE TRADE

Scientists believe that humans first appeared in Africa about 2 million years ago. From there, early humans traveled the Earth, leaving **evidence** of the way they lived behind. Archaeologists know about past life because they study artifacts and remains. Many past civilizations have been discovered and studied over the past 200 years because of hard-working archaeologists. Many more civilizations are waiting to be uncovered.

How do archaeologists know where to look for past life? First they look in and around old ruins. The pyramids in Egypt, the **megalithic**, or stone, monuments in England, and the Temple of Athena in Greece are all ruins that are easy to see.

Another way archaeologists look for past life is by viewing the landscape. They look for strange or unnatural **formations**. Many hills of the same size could be a group of burial mounds. Taking photos from an airplane is very helpful in locating hills and stone patterns on the ground.

Modern digs are different from **excavations** of the 1800s. Scientists working 200 years ago could not take photos from the air. They didn't use tools like the **periscope** or the **magnetometer.** Now archaeologists use a periscope to view areas that are not directly in front of them. They use a magnetometer to measure the strength of the Earth's magnetic field. A magnetometer helped archaeologists in the 1990s when they excavated Troy, an ancient Greek city located in present-day Turkey.

An ancient column is measured at a dig site.

Sometimes archaeologists don't have to search for a dig site. Sometimes the site is found by accident. For example, many construction workers and farmers have found artifacts like bones, stone tools, and pottery pieces. They bring artifacts to scientists. Then scientists can decide if they want to begin a dig. Caves hidden in a jungle, **tombs** buried in a desert, flat grassy plains, and even the ocean floor are all places scientists have found dig sites. The world of archaeology is as big as the world itself!

People work together as a team on a dig. The team members include scientists, students, and volunteers. They use tools to help them search for treasure from the past. Some tools are as small and simple as dental picks and measuring tapes. Other tools are larger and more complicated, like computers, microscopes, magnetometers, and others types of machines.

THE EARLY BRONZE AGE

Scientists often refer to three "ages" when they speak of artifacts. The first age is the Stone Age, the second is the Bronze Age, and the third is the Iron Age.

The Bronze Age is a term that archaeologists use to describe the **prehistoric** period. Prehistoric people used bronze to make their tools. Bronze is a mixture of copper and tin. Civilizations that used bronze made very good use of it. Tools and weapons were probably the most important objects people made. Bronze was also used for cooking pots and art work.

The Bronze Age did not happen at the same time for all cultures around the world. Some cultures did not have copper or tin. Others did not have the skills to make bronze. Copper was the first metal used by humans. Then different cultures learned about bronze through trade, or they developed bronze themselves. Some cultures skipped using copper and moved right into the Bronze Age.

The Aegean civilization was a Bronze Age culture on the Greek island of Crete. The age lasted between 3000 and 1000 BC. During the early Bronze Age, the Minoan *(muh NOH uhn)* civilization was living on Crete. The Minoan civilization was at its height between 2300 and 1500 BC.

What we know of the Minoan culture comes from a palace discovered in 1900. Archaeologist Sir Arthur Evans found the ruin and named it the Palace of Minos *(MY nuhs)*. Minos was a king from Greek **myths.** Minos ruled the entire island of Crete. Knossos *(NAHS uhs)* is the name of the ancient city where the palace ruins are located.

These huge handmade pots were used in ancient times to store olive oil.

Workers help repair a part of an ancient Greek temple.

Arthur Evans continued to dig for several years after the discovery. He uncovered a six-acre palace complex. The Palace of Minos had more than 1,400 rooms. Some rooms were royal apartments. Other rooms were probably used as temples—places to worship. One room, the throne room, was highly decorated and had one large seat higher than the rest. The palace had many rooms, courtyards, passages, stairways, and basements.

Evans worked to rebuild parts of the palace. The work he did 100 years ago has visitors today imagining royal life in the ancient city of Knossos.

Ancient Greeks used gutters and waterspouts on the roofs of temples. The spouts were often shaped like a lion's head and the water drained from its mouth.

Crete was home to about 90 Minoan cities. Hundreds of Minoan sites have been discovered on the island. They range from palace complexes to small towns. Artifacts from the island include pottery and stone vases, gold and silver jewelry, and clay **tablets** that show the ancient Minoan writing called **Linear A.** Artifacts found at the palaces and around the ancient cities are on display at the Iraklion *(ee RAH klee awn)* Museum on Crete.

This is an aerial view of an archaeological work camp.

Colorful Minoan wall paintings can be seen at the Palace of Minos at Knossos on Crete.

Rebuilt and repainted columns stand out among the ruins of the Palace of Minos.

GREEK MYTHS
AND LEGENDS

A myth is a story that tells about a culture's beliefs. Myths tell the stories of people and sometimes imaginary creatures, too. They also include **supernatural** beings like gods and goddesses. Greek myths are about gods and goddesses, their sisters, brothers, mothers, fathers, and children.

A legend is a story that has been passed on for many **generations.** Legends tell about a person or a place. Legends have no real proof of ever happening, but people usually believe them.

Greek myths were a big part of ancient Greek cultures and their history. Greek myths date back to about 2000 BC. Ancient Greeks had their own beliefs and often adopted beliefs from other cultures, too. The result was that many myths were passed on to new cultures, such as the Romans.

Ancient Greeks believed that gods controlled every part of their lives. Greek myths are about the gods of the heavens and how they treated the humans on Earth.

According to Greek myths, Mount Olympus was home to the Greek gods. Mount Olympus is located on the mainland. It is the highest peak in Greece. It rises 9,570 feet (2,917 m) from the Aegean coastline. Read on to learn some strange and interesting facts about some of the gods.

*D*elphi was an ancient Greek holy city. The ancient Greeks thought Delphi was the center of the world. These ruins are of the Oracle Temple.

These decorated columns are part of the Temple of Zeus in Athens.

Titans

The Titans *(TY tuhnz)* were the 12 children of heaven and Earth. Titan Rhea was the mother of the Greek gods.

Zeus

Zeus *(ZOOS)*, son of Rhea, was the leader of the Greek gods. He was the ruler of heaven and Earth. Zeus controlled the weather and his weapon was a lighting bolt. Zeus had children with goddesses and human women.

Poseidon

Poseidon *(puh SY den)* was a brother of Zeus. He was the powerful god of the sea. He fought many battles. His weapon was a three-pronged spear called a trident. The **Mycenaean** people from the late Bronze Age worshiped Poseidon as their chief god.

Hermes

Hermes *(HER meez)* was the son of Zeus and Maia. Maia was the daughter of Titan Atlas. Hermes had many jobs. He protected flocks and shepherds. He guided and protected travelers. Hermes had wings on his back and on the backs of his sandals. He carried a shepherd's hook.

Helen of Troy

Geek myths tell us Helen of Troy was the daughter of Zeus and Leda, a human woman. She was the most beautiful woman in Greece.

Aphrodite

Aphrodite *(af roh DY tee)* was the goddess of love. Aphrodite helped kidnap Helen of Troy, which caused the Trojan War.

Ares

Ares *(AIR eez)* was the god of war. He took the side of the Trojans in the Trojan War. Ares had many children with the goddess Aphrodite.

According to Greek myth, Poseidon was the god of the sea. His marble temple overlooks the beautiful waters off Cape Sounion, south of Athens.

This market place dates back to 500 BC. The ancient Greeks called their marketplace "Agora."

Hera

Hera *(HAIR uh)* was married to Zeus. She was the queen of the Greek gods. Ancient Greeks worshiped Hera as the goddess of marriage, women, and childbirth.

Hephaestus

Hephaestus *(huh FES tus)* was the god of fire. According to Greek poets, Hephaestus was lame, or crippled. One story tells of how he became crippled. Zeus fought with Hephaestus' mother Hera and Hephaestus took sides with his mother. Zeus got angry and knocked Hephaestus off Olympus. Another story tells that Hephaestus was born lame. Hera hated the fact that her son was lame, and out of anger she flung him from the mountain.

This aerial view shows a section of Troy with a Roman-style theater.

The female-figured columns on the Porch of the Erectheum are copies.
The originals were moved to the Acropolis Museum to preserve them.

Demeter

Demeter *(dih MEE tur)* was a sister of Zeus and the goddess of agriculture, or farming. She controlled how crops grew. Myths tell how Demeter forgot the crops. She was upset that her daughter had been kidnaped by Hades, who was god of the underworld, also known as Pluto. Demeter did not care if the world was in danger of starving while her daughter was gone. Zeus fixed that problem by making sure Demeter's daughter spent 6 months with Hades and 6 months with Demeter. From that point on the earth had seasons, like summer and winter.

Artemis

Artemis *(AHR tuh mis)* was the goddess of the hunt and protector of women. It was her job to make sure women had a painless and quick death. Ancient Greeks believed that if a woman died quickly, and without pain, it was because she had been struck by one of Artemis' silver arrows.

Athena

Athena *(uh THEE nuh)* is one of the most famous names in Greek mythology. Athena was the goddess of Athens, the present-day Greek capital city. Athena was born from the forehead of Zeus. She was his favorite child. Athena was a warrior who carried a spear. The famous ancient temple Parthenon *(PAR thuh nahn)* in Athens was built for Athena—the Warrior Maiden.

The Parthenon is made of white marble. It is a temple built for Athena—the Warrior Maiden.

P268   A08/09.0062.005

P393   A08/09.0085.004

P351   A08/09.0008

P352   A08/09.0024.002

P367   A08/09.0062.002

Archaeologists label every artifact.

33

The Parthenon is the largest building on the **acropolis** of Athens. Acropolis is a Greek term that describes the highest point of the city. Most ancient Greek cities had an acropolis. It was the best place to build temples and other important buildings. It was also the safest place because the acropolis was the last place attacked by an enemy.

The Temple of Artemis in present-day Turkey is one of the Seven Wonders of the World.

THE LEGEND OF TROY

In the late Bronze Age, the strongest Greek civilizations were located on the mainland. Around 1400 BC, Mycenae *(my SEE nee)* was the center of the ancient Greek world. The Minoan civilizations on Crete had lost their power.

Mycenae was home to the legendary King Agamemnon *(ag uh MEM nahn)*. Greek myths list Agamemnon as the leader of the Greeks in the Trojan War. Many stories have been written about Agamemnon and the Trojan War. Not all of them seem to be true. One story says that when Agamemnon was sailing across the Aegean Sea to Troy, he sacrificed his daughter to the gods to have wind for his ship.

Greek myths say the Trojan War lasted 10 years. Homer's Iliad describes the last year, when Greek hero Achilles killed Hector, a great Trojan warrior. After Hector's death, the Greeks felt they had won. However, the Greek soldier Odysseus had a plan for one final surprise attack on the Trojans. The Greeks left a huge wooden horse outside the gates of Troy. Inside the horse were Greek soldiers, hiding and waiting for the the right moment to attack. The Trojans dragged the horse into the city. The Greeks sprung out of the horse and the final battle began. The Greeks defeated the Trojans and kidnapped some of their women.

This huge wooden horse is a copy of the legendary Trojan horse. It stands at Troy.

Troy is now a famous archaeological dig site near Hissarlik, Turkey. Excavations have been going on at Troy since its discovery in 1870 by archaeologist Heinrich Schliemann. Schliemann headed digs at Troy for 20 years. Schliemann, and archaeologists who followed him, compared findings at the Tojan ruins with the war stories and poems by Homer. They believe that Homer's stories of the Trojan War may be true. The war probably happened during the 12th century BC.

The ruins of Troy have layers of cities built on top of each other. Each layer is separated by soil and ash. Schliemann destroyed upper layers to get to deeper, older ones. Many scientists didn't like what Schliemann did. However, Schliemann wanted to get to the bottom layers where he would find the Troy Homer wrote about. During his excavations, Schliemann found many gold and silver treasures including earrings, headdresses, bracelets, and thousands of gold beads. Schliemann thought the treasures he found were those of King Priam, the king of Troy during the Trojan War. As it turned out, the layer from which the treasures were taken dated between 2500 and 2200 BC—a time far earlier than the Trojan War.

Other Ancient Greek Treasures

Mycenae and other towns of ancient Greece are now places of great interest to archaeologists. Mycenae was home to ancient stone walls and the well-known Lions Gate. The gate is decorated with two lions facing each other. Through the gate is an area of graves from the 16th century BC. Heinrich Schliemann excavated the graves in 1876. He found treasures of gold. Some of the tombs are called beehive tombs because of their shape. The Treasury of Atreus is the largest tomb at the site. It is believed to be from the 13th century BC.

Around the 13th century BC the Dark Ages began. This is when the Mycenaean civilization fell. Greek people, called the Dorians, took over the southern mainland. The Mycenaean people left the mainland and settled in Ionia (now Turkey). It took several hundred years for people to build new cities on both sides of the Aegean Sea.

The city of Athens became an important center for the Greeks about 500 BC. You can see the ruins of the Parthenon, the Temple of Nike, and the **Erechtheum** on the acropolis. The Parthenon was built about 447 BC. The temple was rectangular with eight columns on the short sides and 17 columns on the long sides. In 1687 part of the temple was destroyed in battle. In 1922 Greek archaeologists began to rebuild some of the columns. The Temple of Nike was named for Athena Nike, the Greek goddess of victory. This temple was much smaller than the Parthenon. It had only four columns on the front. The Temple of Erechtheum was more complex. It had two levels. Rooms on the lower level were dedicated to Poseidon and other gods. The upper level was dedicated to Athena Polias—protector of the city.

This gate is famous for its two lions facing each other at the top. It is located at Mycenae, which was excavated by Heinrich Schliemann in 1876.

*A*ncient decorated columns and arches are among the ruins at Olympia.
Olympia was where the first Olympic Games were held in 776 BC.

West of Athens is the home of the ancient city Olympia. Olympia was the birthplace of the Olympic Games. Historical records say the games began in 776 BC. However, some believe the games were played much earlier. The ruins at Olympia include parts of buildings' foundations and statues. Records show that the Temple of Hera, the Temple of Zeus, the stadium, the race track, and the gymnasium were among the important buildings at Olympia. The beautiful and historical Greek ruins have given scientists a great way to piece together what was fact and what was myth.

The science of archaeology has taught us a great deal about ancient Greece, but there are still many unknowns. It is up to future archaeologists to study these unknowns.

PLACES AND NAMES PRONUNCIATION GUIDE

Places:

acropolis *(uh KRAHP uh lis)*

Aegean *(eh JEE uhn)*

Balkan *(BALL kin)*

Crete *(KREET)*

Iraklion *(ee RAH klee awn)*

Knossos *(NAHS uhs)*

Mycenae *(my SEE nee)*

Parthenon *(PAR thuh nahn)*

People:

Agamemnon *(ag uh MEM nahn)*

Aphrodite *(af roh DY tee)*

Ares *(AIR eez)*

Artemis *(AHR tuh mis)*

Athena *(uh THEE nuh)*

Demeter *(dih MEE tur)*

Hephaestus *(huh FES tus)*

Hera *(HAIR uh)*

Hermes *(HER meez)*

Minoan *(muh NOH uhn)*

Minos *(MY nuhs)*

Poseidon *(puh SY den)*

Titans *(TY tuhnz)*

Zeus *(ZOOS)*

GLOSSARY

acropolis (eh KRAHP eh lis) — the highest and most
defensible part of a Greek city

archaeologist (AR kee AHL uh jest) — a person who studies
past human life by studying artifacts left by ancient people

artifacts (ART eh fakts) — objects made or changed
by humans

Erechtheum (ih REK thee um) — a temple dedicated to
Erectheus who was King of Athens and raised by
goddess Athena

evidence (EV e dens) — anything that can be used as proof

excavations (EK skeh VAY shunz) — removing earth
by digging

formations (for MAY shunz) — formed structures or shapes

generations (JEN eh RAY shunz) — single steps in the line
of ancestors

Linear A (LIN ee er AY) — a writing script used by the
Minoan culture beginning in the 19th century BC.

magnetometer (MAG neh TOM eh ter) — an instrument used
to measure the Earth's magnetic field

megalithic (MEG eh LITH ik) — huge stone prehistoric
monuments

Mycenaean (my SEE nee in) — people from Mycenae

GLOSSARY

myths (MITHS) — imaginary stories that tell of a culture's beliefs and involve creatures and supernatural beings such as gods

periscope (PAIR ih skohp) — a tube-like instrument that allows someone to see something that they might not be able to see, such as around a corner, or on another level above or below

prehistoric (PREE hi STOR ik) — a time before written history

ruins (ROO enz) — the remains of something that has been destroyed

supernatural (SOO per NACH er al) — beyond what is natural; relating to the spirit world

tablets (TAB lits) — slabs used for inscriptions (stone or clay)

tombs (TOOMS) — places for burial

FURTHER READING

The Young Oxford Book of Archaeology ©1997 Norah Moloney, Oxford University Press, NY

Archeology, Eyewitness Books ©1994 Dr. Jane McIntosh, Alfred A. Knopf, Inc., NY

Lost Treasures of the World ©1993 Michael Groushko, Multimedia Books Ltd., London

Lost Cities © 1997 Paul G Bahn, Welcome Rain, New York

Finding the Lost Cities © 1997 Rebecca Steoff, Oxford University Press, NY

Ancient Greece, Eyewitness Books © 1992 Anne Pearson, Alfred A. Knopf, Inc., NY

Encarta Encyclopedia © 1996 Microsoft Corporation

Grolier Multimedia Encyclopedia ©1998 Grolier Inc.

The Acropolis of Athens
   www.geocities.com/athens/oracle/1039/index.html

Sir Arthur Evans/Crete Minoan Site
   www.dilos.com/region/crete/evans.html

Minoan Crete Site
   www.uk.digiserve.com/menton/minoan/index.html

INDEX

acropolis   34, 40
  at Athens   34, 40, 43
Aegean Sea   5, 22, 36, 40
Agamemnon   7, 36
Athens   7, 32, 34, 40
Balkan peninsula   5
beehive tombs   39
Bronze Age   13, 14, 25, 35
Crete   5, 14, 18
Evans, Sir Arthur   14, 17
Greek gods   21, 22, 25, 26,
  28, 31, 32, 36
Greek myths   21, 22, 25, 26,
  28, 31, 32, 36
Homer   7, 8, 36, 38
Ionian Sea   5
Knossos   7, 14, 17
Mediterranean Sea   5

Minoan culture   7, 14, 18, 35
Minos, King   14
Palace of Minos   7, 14, 17
Mount Olympus   22, 28
Mycenae   7, 35, 36, 39
Mycenaean culture   7, 40
Olympia   7, 43
Olympic Games   7, 43
Parthenon   7, 32, 34, 40
Priam, King   38
Schliemann, Heinrich   38,
  39
Trojan War   26, 36, 38
Troy   7, 10, 26, 35, 36, 38